STARTING A
YOUTH MINISTRY

BY LARRY KEEFAUVER

Group
Books

P.O. Box 481 ● Loveland, CO 80539

STARTING A YOUTH MINISTRY

Copyright © 1984 by Larry Keefauver

Second Printing

Library of Congress Catalog No. 84-80321
ISBN 0936-664-19-3

Credits
Designed by Jean Bruns
Cover illustration by Laurel Watson

CONTENTS

Dedicated to the Lord Jesus Christ and the youth and youth sponsors through whom he has touched my life over the years.

FOREWORD

The most challenging step in most endeavors is simply
getting started. Starting a youth group (or revitalizing a
dormant one) requires energy and tenacity. But energy
and tenacity need to be directed into the right channel
for effective youth ministry. That's why I am pleased to
recommend this **Starting a Youth Ministry** resource by
Larry Keefauver.

Larry draws from his tremendous experience,
organized mind, and compassion for youth to offer this
concise, expertly developed and well-conceived
"recipe" for getting started in youth ministry.

Many people I have met across the country in training events, workshops, seminars and youth rallies have
been saying the same thing, "If I just knew how to
begin." Well, now they can.

Larry has done a masterful job of getting to the point
for the leader who has little time to spend wading
through theoretical religious material. Yet, when you
read and begin to follow Larry's thoughts, you discover
a common-sense approach to beginning and maintaining
a youth group. This approach is prefaced with loving
the Lord and the young people. If you do that and follow
some basic guidelines—you will not fail. That thought
has to be comforting to those of you in the role of starting or revitalizing a youth group.

As the book opens, you immediately will begin to see
some of the available tools for evaluating where you are
and where your group is. As you complete the inven-
tories and test some of the models, your anxiety level

will diminish and you will be more open to follow some of the other described courses of action.

Starting a Youth Ministry is a handbook and a manual. Treat it in that manner. Do not read it as a novel, but work with the first chapter. Then proceed to the other chapters as you determine your needs. Keep **Starting a Youth Ministry** on your desk or bed table and refer to it periodically for specifics. When you have the basic elements for doing youth ministry, it's natural that you will look to program ideas. Included here are chapters on programs and building your own support group. If I have learned anything in the past 22 years in youth ministry, it is that each of us desperately needs some-one else—a life-support system. If we don't have this backup, then we eventually wear away into a condition known as burnout.

Realizing the hunger, the constant turnover in leader-ship and the apparent apathy among the young for youth ministry, Larry has combined his organizational skills and faith with a well-developed educational proc-ess that is easily understood.

I recommend **Starting a Youth Ministry.** You will benefit from these pages of serious and faithful content spiced with real-life stories and anecdotes.

—J. David Stone

INTRODUCTION

Fifteen years ago I had the exciting experience of graduating from seminary and entering my first pastorate. As an associate minister, I had the opportunity to work with the young people as well as in many other ministries in the church. Unfortunately, little of my graduate education was devoted specifically to youth ministry. At that time, there were few books and only random theories about how to work with young people in the church setting. Most of what was done was recreational. It was exciting to meet with other associate ministers in my district and region just to learn crowd-breakers and activities. Then came Lyman Coleman's "Serendipity" workshops. These offered practical youth ministry ideas. It was invigorating as everyone rushed from one Serendipity workshop to the next, grabbing new ideas and insights. Other groups and training opportunities came on the scene and gradually more resources and ideas were shared nationwide in youth ministry.

From learning to work the trial-and-error method in the local church to the more formal process of training and equipping youth ministers, and through talking with thousands of other youth ministry people across the country in J. David Stone's "Rainbow" workshops, I have developed my own principles. These principles for working with young people and specifically in starting a youth ministry in the local congregation seem to be fairly universal. Such basic directions are important to move from getting together just for the fun of it to a systematic plan of reaching all young people.

I hope to help you avoid some of the pitfalls and mistakes that I made over the years and enable you to build a solid foundation for youth ministry in your congregation. Whether you are a volunteer youth worker or a youth ministry professional, these principles will help you discover the basic steps you need to take to develop a lasting youth ministry program in your congregation.

One important step is never try to begin or revive a youth ministry by yourself. A support team of adults and young people is necessary to assist you. Whether you belong to a large church or a small church, this team should be instituted with the sole responsibility of organizing and implementing a youth ministry.

All ideas presented in **Starting a Youth Ministry** can be adapted—whatever the size of your church. If you have a small church, incorporate one adult, one parent and one young person to work with you when you first begin. If your church is larger, increase the numbers of your support team. Remember to be flexible and use the ideas presented in this resource to fit your particular situation.

If the youth ministry is properly developed, it can become ongoing—no matter who in the church works with the program. It will not matter which new professionals are brought in or which volunteers quit.

One congregation I served in central Texas had had a succession of youth ministry assistants and interns with a turnover about every six months during a 10-year period. The youth in that church had never experienced a far-reaching, systematic, long-term youth ministry program. No foundation had ever been built, because each intern or youth ministry assistant had relied on his or her own personal way of doing things. The youth ministry in the congregation was built around the personality of the particular leader. As a result, the youth had become disenchanted with youth ministry in the church. The young people didn't know who to trust or what was going to happen next. So they stopped attending. It took more than 18 months to build the kind of trust and rapport needed to re-establish youth ministry in that congregation.

If youth ministry has a solid foundation and is a priority in the church's ministry, then an ongoing program such as the one described in these pages can help you maintain an ebullient youth ministry.

I want to acknowledge the tremendous help that I have had over the past 15 years in youth ministry. As I have developed these principles, my deepest appreciation goes to my wife, Judy, and to my family. They have been patient and supportive of me during the many weekend retreats, lock-ins and activities that took me away from home. I also am deeply indebted to J. David Stone who encouraged and supported me through the years in youth ministry and who offered me many valuable comments and criticisms regarding this manuscript. I want to acknowledge the hard work, typing and editing by Gloria Frogge, and the editorial efforts of Sandra Wilmoth, Cindy Hansen and Lee Sparks at Group Books.

These ideas are not just mine but come from the thousands of people whom I have met during the past five years at the Rainbow workshops, as we led youth ministry training countrywide through the Youth Ministries Counsultation Service. To both young people and adults, I express my deepest appreciation for the shared ideas, affirmation and confirmation of many of the principles in this book. And to those in each of the churches that I have served and who have worked with me as volunteers and shared with me in the youth groups in Texas at the First Christian Church, Waxahachie; First Christian Church, Lubbock; Central Christian Church, Waco; and in Florida at the First Christian Church, Tampa; and the Parkway Christian Church in Plantation. I express my deepest love for their patience and understanding of me as I grew in ministry.

Finally, it is my prayer that the reader will discover tools and skills to enable the love of Jesus Christ to touch youth, so that God receives glory and people are brought closer to the living Christ.

CHAPTER ONE
If Not You, Who?

So now you've done it. You have decided to start or revive the youth program in your congregation. Congratulations! You are special, for within you are all the gifts and talents necessary to reach out and enrich the lives of others through Jesus Christ. I know this is an exciting and scary decision you have made. The purpose of this book is simple: to help you do what you have decided to do.

Many churches have never had a youth ministry program. In other churches, the youth ministry program has dwindled to nothing. The young people who were participating have drifted away. Interest lags and apathy abounds. A new start is needed. An initiator is essential. Remember the saying: If not here, where? If not now, when? If not you, who?

You are the person to make that youth ministry happen.

How did it happen to be you? The following checklist includes various situations related to youth workers. Check the situation(s) that most closely parallels your circumstances:

Situations

_____I'm relatively new in this church and I'm young. I suppose I appear to be a likely candidate to work with the young people and pastor. Besides, the education committee invited me to help out, so here I am.

_____ I like working with young people.

_____ I want to donate some of my time to the church, and this seems to be a fun area.

_____ We're a young couple with children of our own, but there is no one else to do the job. In fact, we were told if we didn't do it, it wouldn't get done.

_____ I have just been hired as the youth minister or staff person in charge of youth programming for our church.

_____ I am a parent of one of the teenagers in the church. If I don't do something, my child will not have a youth program. I have to get something done.

_____ I feel God is guiding me in this direction.

_____ Other (explain): _____

No matter which situation(s) you find yourself in, you still may wonder: "How can I be sure I am suited for youth ministry as either a volunteer or a professional? Will anybody help me? What is the church willing to do to assure that youth ministry will succeed? How do I know where to begin in planning a youth ministry? What steps do I take?"

As you read this book, we are going to discover together your unique abilities to do youth ministry and some practical step-by-step actions that you can take to get the job done. Regardless of the circumstances in which you are involved, two things are essential—that you like working with young people and you believe that God is calling you to this service.

YOUR MOTIVATIONS

One of the first steps in beginning a youth ministry is for you to come to grips with why it interests you and what you have to offer. In other words, you must understand your motivation before you leap into the exciting ministry for youth.

The following is a list of possible incentives which prompted you to work with the young people in your congregation. Rank them from 1 to 10, with 1 the foremost reason you were motivated and 10 your least likely incentive:

Incentives

1._____The pastor was desperate, so I agreed. I felt I couldn't let the pastor down. Besides, I wanted affirmation and approval.

2._____I'm upset that the youth do not know more about the Bible and the Christian faith.

3._____I have volunteered to be certain that they learn the correct theology.

4._____I find it easier to work and relate with young people than with other adults.

5._____These young people can be my friends and my support group.

6._____I want to feel needed by the church.

7._____I have been feeling guilty about doing so little in our congregation.

8._____I simply couldn't say "no" when they asked me, but I feel very tentative and ambivalent about being a group leader. I feel bad when I say "no."

9._____When this opportunity came along, I jumped at it because it adequately fulfills my need of servanthood.

10._____I believe that God is leading me to do this and wants me to serve him in this manner.

11._____I love young people and have enjoyed positive relationships with them in the past.

12._____I want to share with others how tremendous God has been in my life.

13._____I believe I can make a significant contribution here and use my talents and skills to serve others.

14._____I really feel good about myself, am growing as a Christian and desire to share Christ with others.

15._____I want young people to feel good about themselves and to grow in their faith.

Look at the statements above. The first nine statements are self-centered. How many of these were in your top five reasons for being in youth ministry? These statements mean your motivation for being in youth ministry has more to do with your own needs than the needs of others.

Now reread statements 10 through 15. These are centered on the needs of others. How many of these statements were in your top five reasons for being in youth ministry? Compare this to the self-centered statements.

If your top five reasons for being in youth ministry were more self-centered than other-centered, you need to further re-examine your motives for wanting to work with young people. Being centered and focused on the needs of others more than on ourselves is a more positive, reinforcing reason for being in youth work.

I recall one individual who years ago had entered youth ministry because she was lonely and lacked positive affirmation from her family and other adult friends. She loved the young people; she would have them to her house during the week and on weekends take them on special trips. Sometimes, she did more with the teenagers than with her own family. As time went on, certain young people in the group related well to this woman. Eventually, they became so close that others in the group felt left out. A clique was formed. Certain group members met the particular needs of this youth sponsor while others did not. As a result, tremendous friction and problems developed within the youth themselves and also among the other sponsors.

If we enter youth ministry for the purpose of getting our own needs met, there will come a point that our needs are destructive to the youth group.

It is important to remember that ministry is giving ourselves to others. If we work to meet the needs of the young people, we will find tremendous benefit. "Whatever a man sows, that he will also reap" (Galatians 6:7). When we sow love, we reap love. When we sow ministry, we receive ministry from others.

What Can You Do?

You have taken one of the first steps in beginning a youth ministry, you have made the commitment and you have the motivation. Another important step is for you to identify those kinds of things that you enjoy most and do best. One of the keys to youth ministry is to *not* do something you dislike. Many people can contribute to youth ministry. You don't have to do everything yourself. Still, you need to know what you do best.

Following are directions and a checklist of possibilities for working with youth and the tasks involved. Discover what you do best.

● Rate each of the items 1 to 4. One means you enjoy the activity very much, 2—okay, 3—not so well, 4—don't enjoy the activity at all.

● Put asterisks by those areas in which you would like to learn more.

● Put arrows by those jobs that you would need to find someone else to do.

Abilities

_____Plan and organize activities

_____Prepare a calendar and a schedule

_____Evaluate past events and quickly understand what's happening

_____Change and revise what's happening in mid-course, if necessary

_____Follow Christian education and youth ministry goals and objectives

_____Handle and resolve conflicts constructively

_____Positively persuade and influence others

_____Publicize and promote youth activities

_____Generate enthusiasm

_____Teach youth

_____Affirm and appreciate youth and other adults

_____Create new and exciting ideas and dreams

_____See needed or coming change and plan ahead

_____Inspire and motivate others

_____Tackle problems with energy

_____Anticipate and eagerly look toward the future

_____Solve problems creatively

_____Make detailed arrangements for evening fellowships and events

_____Accurately sense and feel the mood of youth

_____Work patiently with others

_____Enjoy seeing plans implemented and working well

_____Adapt well to changes in program

_____Relaxed and casual with youth

_____Like to follow a plan or schedule

_____Able to get things thought out and thoroughly organized

_____Practical, realistic and systematic

_____Comfortable with rules and discipline or being an authority figure

_____Feel good about leading programs or events

_____Advocate for youth ministry to church committees and councils

_____Able to form the best concept, idea or reason for doing things

_____Comfortable one-on-one

_____At ease in front of a group

_____Like to research ideas and resources for youth ministry

Review your responses. Celebrate the statements you numbered 1 or 2. These are areas in which you already have strengths.

Identify those things you need to learn, then find others to support you by doing those tasks that you do not enjoy. In Chapter 3 we will study means to build support.

Contemplate this passage: "I can do all things in him who strengthens me" (Philippians 4:13). Pause a moment. Reflect on all those things that you can do. Thank God for this opportunity to work with teenagers as you get ready for this wonderful, new adventure in your life.

God, thank you for giving me the talent to help me accomplish some of what I need to do. Give me the courage to seek new knowledge and skills for working with youth. Grant me the power to

reach out to others who can help me do what I cannot do. God, I praise you for this opportunity to work with youth. Amen.

CHAPTER TWO
Have a Purpose

Before starting or reviving a youth ministry in your congregation, it is important to have a purpose in mind. This step should be taken at least six months before beginning the youth ministry. Take a moment to think of your reason for starting or reviving a youth group. In the following space, write in one sentence the purpose of youth ministry as you understand it:

_____

_____

As I have traveled across the country and visited with thousands of youth ministers, volunteer youth workers and pastors, they have stated various purposes for having a youth group:

"Every church ought to have a youth group."

"The pastor wanted one."

"The church down the street has a big youth ministry. We have to try to keep up."

"Too many of our kids are going to clubs and groups at school. We need to balance that with Christian church groups."

"The parents in our congregation insisted that we offer something to their children."

"It is a good evangelistic tool to recruit other youth and families to the church."

Was your purpose similar to some of these? While there may be some positive motives behind these rationalizations, they are generally superficial. We need to explore more fully our ultimate purpose for youth ministry.

Most purposes are centered on one of three concepts: "in"stitution, "in"dividual or "in" Christ.

"In"stitution

Many youth groups are started or revived because of church pressure. The pastor, the leadership or a committee within the congregation desires youth ministry for the church. These are some positive reasons for beginning a youth ministry based on institutional pressure or necessity:

● If the group is centered on the institution, it will receive funding and support from the leadership and congregation.

● The institution can lend its vitality and emotional support to the group.

● The institution can set long-term goals and objectives for the direction of the group.

However, there are pitfalls to an institutional center:

● The institution may be more interested in meeting its own needs than the needs of the youth.

● The leadership of the institution may not always be sensitive to the directions and programming needed for youth ministry to succeed.

● What the institution gives, the institution can take away. It is not unusual for churches to pull support from youth ministry as quickly as it was offered.

"In"dividual

Centering the purpose of youth ministry on an individual can take a number of forms. Churches and youth ministries sometimes seek to build programs around a charismatic person whose personal magnetism can attract followers. Thus, the church will hire an exciting and dynamic person to work with youth or will seek out an enthusiastic lay volunteer.

Youth ministry programs also sometimes build the entire group around a few young people within the membership. Strong youth can demand certain directions for youth ministry and may threaten to withdraw from the group if their demands and needs are not met.

A youth ministry program also can be built around a parent. Some parents claim to know what is best for their own children and church youth ministry. While they may have strong, positive ideas, one person should never dictate the direction of an entire youth ministry in a church. One thing you need to check is whether or not you are that individual. Are you the one who has demanded that the congregation have youth ministry? Or are you the one around whom the congregation is seeking to build a youth program?

Here are some advantages to centering a program on the individual:

● A single person often is more efficient and can get things moving quickly and effectively.

● Strong, positive personalities can attract young people and persuade parents and other adults in the congregation to support youth ministry.

● A single person can be the focal point for publicizing and making youth ministry highly visible within the congregation.

Although there are immediate benefits in centering youth ministry on an individual, there are shortcomings:

● An individual may be programming to meet his or her needs in youth ministry, rather than meeting the needs of the youth.

● An individual who senses a popular following may become increasingly authoritarian and uncooperative with other leaders and church committees.

● The program can grow to be too large for one person to handle effectively.

● When the individual moves on to other kinds of ministries or leaves the congregation, the program built around him or her will falter and possibly fail.

"In" Christ

The most successful way to start a youth group is to begin with Christ at the center. He needs to be at the center of your life, your congregation and your ministry. With Christ at the center, individual needs can be met through the ministry of the entire youth group and ultimately the whole congregation. Christ's power is available for your ministry—be sure to seek it in humility and praise. "If any one is in Christ, he is a new creation; the old has passed away, behold, the new has come" (2 Corinthians 5:17). In Ephesians, Paul offers more exhortations to build our ministries in Christ. "So then you are no longer strangers and sojourners, but you are fellow citizens with the saints and members of the household of God, built upon the foundation of the apostles and prophets, Christ Jesus himself being the cornerstone, in whom the whole structure is joined together and grows into a holy temple in the Lord; in whom you also are built into it for a dwelling place of God in the Spirit" (Ephesians 2:19-22).

If Christ is at the center, the group can be both inclusive and outreaching. The following diagram illustrates the term inclusive:

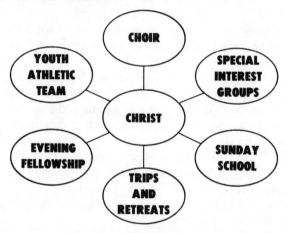

With your youth group placing Christ in the center of its ministry, future conflict can be forestalled. If an institution, individual or activity enters the center circle, competition and conflict are inevitable. For example, in a number of congregations the youth choir and the evening fellowship are in constant conflict. They are vying to be at the center of youth ministry either as groups or through strong charismatic individuals who are leaders of those groups. If both groups and leaders are centered on Christ and are working together as one body in Christ, then communication is possible.

20

Working together as the body of Christ also facilitates an outreaching ministry to teenagers. As you begin working with youth, you will discover there are some youth who will want to participate in everything that is offered. Others will only relate to those aspects of the youth program that meet their needs. They may attend a trip or retreat but ignore all other programs. Others may only come to Sunday school. Some may be in the choir or a music program, but not in the evening fellowship. Still others will only relate to a church athletic team, but not to any other function. Our tendency is to want to exclude those who only have one particular need met. For example, if the young person only plays on the church basketball team but does not come to evening fellowship, our ego will often tempt us to exclude that person from other youth group activities.

Let me emphasize that all youth group activities are reaching out for Jesus Christ. If a young person can only be reached and touched by Jesus Christ through the athletic team, we should do nothing to discourage him or her from playing on the team or attending other youth activities. This means, of course, that young people who have worked hard earning money toward a trip or retreat should have first preference to go. But if the young person who has not attended regularly wants to go and is willing to pay his or her fair share, that individual should not be denied the opportunity. Jesus Christ may use that event to touch the life of that young person.

I'll never forget a young man who years ago played on our church basketball team. The church teams were directed by a youth ministry council. The council insisted that all the coaches be Christ-centered and emphasize Christian principles on the sports team. This young person wanted to play on the team, but he was not really active in other ministries of the church such as Sunday school, worship or evening fellowship. The first inclination of the youth ministry leaders was to exclude him from playing on the team. However, he was included on the team. Through the witness of that Christian coach and the love of that Christian basketball team, the young man was brought to the freedom of knowing Jesus Christ.

Youth ministry both "reaches in" to touch everyone involved and "reaches out" to non-Christians to lead them to Christ.

THE BASIS OF YOUTH MINISTRY

Gather the people responsible for organizing or revitalizing the youth ministry for a one-hour plan-the-purpose session. These people will complete and discuss the circle diagram below to clarify the purpose of the youth ministry:

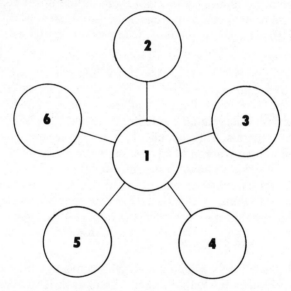

Step one: Following are two lists, one is "people-centered" and the other is "program-centered." Have the potential group leaders fill in the circles in the diagram by choosing items from either the Programs list or the People list. These are to be ranked in order of importance. (Congregations tend to think of youth ministry in terms of programs or people.) Option: The group may choose to fill out two sets of diagrams—one for the People list and another one for the Programs list.

Programs

Church
Sunday school
Youth music
Retreats and trips
Evening fellowship
Special ministries:
   (clown ministry,
   puppetry, drama,
   evangelism, outreach,
   other)

People

Pastor
Associate or youth minister
Adult youth workers
Teachers
Church lay leaders
Parents
Youth group members

Step two: After each individual has filled in the diagram, compare the sheets. Ask the participants where Christ fits in the diagram. How important is Christ in each of the circles? Discuss the changes of priorities and attitudes with programs and people centered on Christ. In youth ministry workshops I have conducted, it is not uncommon for people to realize that they initially rated Christ-centered ministries lower than other activities or people. Emphasize that youth ministry must be in Christ to be effective.

One congregation in Florida filled in the circle diagram as follows:

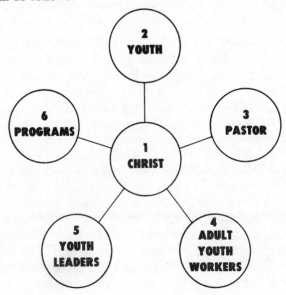

23

The group's leader explained how they arrived at this diagram: "We would put Christ in the center. In the first priority of youth ministry after Christ, we put the youth. We program youth ministry to meet the needs of youth. If their needs are being met, they will want to come and be active. If needs are not being met, they'll go elsewhere.

"Next, we put the pastor. The pastor needs to be included in youth ministry and as a vital part of all that happens. His support, input and guidance are essential. This doesn't mean that he is in control of youth ministry. Jesus is. But it does mean that he is an active, not passive, participant. The rest of those rankings have to do with meeting the needs of youth, so we listed the adult youth workers, youth leaders and programs."

In some congregations, the youth place evening fellowship at a higher priority than Sunday school, music or other ministries. Other churches might emphasize different structures in programming depending upon size, number of volunteers and youth. Such churches may decide to place all the ministries on the outside circles on an equal basis, emphasizing certain events at given times of the year. For example, a mission trip could be emphasized during the summer and choir during Christmas.

Step three: In one sentence, write a purpose for youth ministry that will be adopted by your congregation and understood by all people working with the group, including the youth. Include the teenagers in your congregation in this process so that they contribute and feel an ownership in the final results. Here is an example of a one-sentence youth ministry purpose: "The purpose of youth ministry in our congregation is to provide a small group experience where people (youth and adults) witness, serve and come together in Christian fellowship, much like the New Testament church."

After the meeting, be sure the people directly responsible for youth ministry have a similar understanding of the purpose. It is important that the pastor, staff, committees, and others involved with the youth ministry understand and support the group's purpose.

24

Publicize the purpose and the diagram in the church after both the diagram and written purpose are completed and allow input and ideas from the congregation. Publish these in the church newsletter, brochures and materials given to prospective members.

Now that you have discovered the three possible concepts on which to base the purpose and have learned how to complete a circle diagram, take a moment to review the purpose you wrote at the start of this chapter. Was your purpose centered on individuals or institutions? Was it centered on Christ? Now rewrite your purpose below according to new thoughts gathered from this chapter. (Notice any changes or similarities and the positive and negative effects.)

_____

_____

CHAPTER THREE
Build a Support Team

After you have a purpose clearly in mind, it is important for you to know who will support youth ministry in the congregation.

Form a support team with the pastor, several adults, parents, and young people to help you start or revive a youth ministry.

If your congregation is small, the support team can consist of the pastor, one adult, one parent and one young person. The number of members on the support team should increase with the size of your church.

Some church members may not want to serve on the support team, but will support you with prayers and finances. This type of assistance is also necessary. The important point to remember: Never begin a youth ministry by yourself—involve others.

THE PASTOR

The first person to check with is your pastor; he or she is the key to a successful youth ministry. If the pastor is supportive, youth ministry can be successful. If the pastor does not fully back the youth ministry, then all the efforts may be futile.

About six months before beginning or reviving a youth ministry, meet with your pastor to ascertain if he or she will:

● work with you in identifying and helping to recruit other lay people in the congregation to work with the youth ministry.

● work with your financial committee and church governing board to set up adequate financial support.

● help you visit with parents to secure their support for the congregation's purpose and directions.

● provide ideas and other resources.

● be willing to attend at least one youth meeting or event every month.

● help publicize and promote the youth ministry.

Your pastor's answers to these questions are the first step in building support within the congregation. Without his or her support, youth ministry at best can only exist in a congregation and at worst it will go nowhere.

CHURCH LEADERSHIP

Although leaders within the congregation may not want to serve on the support team, it is important that they fully endorse the purpose, directions and financial undergirding of the youth ministry.

To gain this endorsement, ask your pastor to accompany you on a visit to the lay ministry leadership of your church. If these leaders already have been involved in the initial meeting to establish the purpose of youth ministry, such a visit will be unnecessary.

It is important that the pastor, volunteers, and you clearly state and agree upon the goals for youth ministry in your congregation. To choose and state goals, appoint a spokesman or a panel that includes your pastor. If you choose to have a panel, it is helpful to have possible goals printed and distributed for formation meetings. Or use a blackboard or overhead projector during the planning stages. Some of the goals to share with the panel might include:

● Meet weekly.

● Encourage youth to grow in Christian faith through Bible study and personal sharing.

● Develop positive relationships among the youth and adult sponsors.

● Work actively in the congregation through service projects. Assist the adult leaders of the congregation.

- Sponsor overnight or weekend retreats regularly throughout the year to foster deeper Christian community. Focus on more intensive learning and sharing situations.
- Develop a small group of youth and adults that models the church itself.
- Brainstorm with church leaders and others in the congregation to find those who will work with and support the youth ministry.

Turn to the education committee or official governing group in your congregation for aid in developing a budget and financial support for youth ministry.

Prepare a formula to follow in establishing the youth ministry. You will need funds for some of the following items:

Books and programming resources	$_____
Sunday school curriculum	$_____
Evening youth fellowship	$_____
Retreats and trips	$_____
Snackfood	$_____
Training youth workers	$_____
Total	$_____

It is difficult to estimate exactly how much money you will need for the initial budget, but a good rule for financial planning is to allot from $50 to $100 for each young person each year. This should enable the congregation to support some trips and retreats for the group as well as provide enough program support to get started to undergird the Sunday school and evening fellowship programs. Thus, if you anticipate working with 20 young people in the course of the next year, budget $1,000 to $2,000. It is discouraging to try to do youth ministry without adequate financial support. Presenting fund-raising projects throughout the year becomes debilitating and counterproductive. It is one thing to do some fund raising as a group to give the youth a feeling of ownership and responsibility, but to place the entire financial burden on them can divert the group's focus from Christ to money. The congregation also might become quite weary of continuous fund-raising projects and will be much more supportive in the long run of a few fund-raising projects with a primary emphasis on supporting youth ministry through the church budget. Many congregations plan to subsidize each youth event such as a summer camp or retreat with one-third to one-half of the registration costs. This enables the young people to provide ownership in the event by paying a portion of their way, but it also helps keep the cost down.

In addition to financing from the church budget, contact individuals who have indicated a strong interest in youth ministry. Meet with them to see if they would be willing to give additional support.

You might, however, feel that the financial and volunteer support of the congregation is lacking. The church body might think youth ministry is a great idea, yet be unwilling to commit time or money to help you make youth ministry happen in your church. In my first congregation, we had limited financial resources for our youth ministry program—only a couple hundred dollars. In addition to that, no one was willing to work as a youth sponsor. Everyone had the misconception that because I had been hired to lead youth ministry they could sit back and watch me. Being very frustrated and not knowing where to turn, I asked the parents to show their support by volunteering a month at a time to attend youth meetings and help me in whatever way they could. I knew this would give them the opportunity to see what I was doing in youth ministry and would give me adult support. Their willingness to come a month at a time, even though they couldn't commit for longer periods, gave me enough support and encouragement to continue.

You cannot begin a youth ministry by yourself, you need others. If the congregation is unwilling to give a commitment in any way, then this may not be the best time to start a youth ministry in your congregation. If the congregation really believes that you are sincere in wanting to begin a youth ministry with a solid foundation, I believe there are individuals who will give specific amounts of money or small commitments of time to be there as you get started.

This is the evaluation question that you must answer for yourself, "Does the congregation want me to go it alone, or have they given me enough commitment in time and money to make youth ministry fruitful?" If the answer is one of affirmation, now is the time to gather the parents and begin.

PARENTS AND THE FORMATION MEETING

We have studied ways of involving the pastor and congregation on a youth ministry support team, but what about the parents? How do we go about involving them in youth ministry? After the pastor and the congregational leadership have indicated they will be supportive of youth ministry, plan and schedule a formation meeting for parents.

Begin by sending a letter to all parents indicating the time and place of the first formation meeting. The letter could look like this:

Dear Parent:

We believe youth ministry is going to be a vital and important part of our church's program. Your child is important to God and to us at our church. We need your support to minister effectively to youth in our congregation. Without parental support, youth ministry is impossible. Our purpose for youth ministry is: (Insert the already established and written purpose.)

Our pastor and congregational leadership are in full support of this purpose and have provided $_____ for youth ministry in our church for the coming year. We now want to visit with you about how you can be supportive of youth ministry.

Will you bring a covered dish of _____ and join us in Room _____ on _____(date)_____ at _(time)_ for a dinner and sharing of our mutual love of youth and the importance they are to Jesus Christ in our church.

I shall be calling you soon to see if you can attend.

Yours in Christ,

The letters should be sent to the parents approximately two weeks before the meeting. Also publicize the meeting through your church worship bulletin and newsletter. It is then important that you, the pastor and the others helping you with the youth ministry call the parents to get their commitments to attend. That personal telephone call is critical. Make the telephone calls five or six days before the meeting so that it is close enough to remind the parents of the meeting and yet early enough to give you a reliable count for the number to attend.

Different action works in different situations to prompt parents to attend a formation meeting. Usually the parents are eager and excited about youth ministry in the congregation. They will attend and do anything they are asked to do to be supportive. In some situations, however, the parents worked laboriously with the church leadership until a full- or part-time youth ministry leader was hired. Then, some of these same parents tended to feel that because a leader had been hired, there was no need for further involvement on their part.

One congregation I was in had that kind of attitude. We should have had 75 to 100 parents at the formation meeting, but even after letters, telephone calls and personal invitations, only about 25 parents showed up. As these parents sat with me and we talked about responsibilities and filled out the parent volunteer form, I mulled in my mind, "What do I have to do so that parents know I am really serious about this?"

A few months after the poor turnout at the parents meeting, I went through channels in the church and sent out letters to the parents in the congregation. This letter told them the purpose of youth ministry and the critical importance of their participation. I also had a phrase in the letter that explained, "If you really want your youth to participate in youth ministry in our congregation, your attendance is expected at this meeting." Now that is a strong statement, but it certainly got their attention because it was in capital letters and underlined. The two weeks before the meeting, I made telephone calls personally urging and inviting parents to attend. And if they were unwilling to attend, I asked them for an appropriate time for me or another representative to visit with them. If they weren't willing to attend the formation meeting, we were willing to go to them—sit with them face-to-face, and help them complete the volunteer sheet and talk about the importance of youth ministry for their young person and for the church.

I discovered that when the parents were aware that I was willing to go to them with a calendar, volunteer sheet and all other pertinent information, they made youth ministry a higher priority and started participating in increasing numbers. Support was built and a good relationship was developed. After I got tough with my commitment, parents became realistic about their involvement.

Now that you have an acceptable interest from the parents and an idea of how many will be attending the formation meeting, you need to prepare an agenda. Items on the agenda can include:

Prayer. Offer a prayer thanking God for the time together and the opportunity to begin a youth ministry. Ask for God's blessing and guidance in the meeting and in the months to come.

Food. Include a time for the parents to meet and talk with each other and to enjoy a potluck. If you don't want to have anything as elaborate as a potluck, plan a snacktime. Modify the letter to the parents and invite them to bring crackers, cheese and fruit to the meeting. The church can provide the beverage.

Welcome and introduction. Ask the pastor to give an enthusiastic address on the importance of youth ministry in the church.

The minister can emphasize important statistics that would serve to reinforce the point: A Youth Research Survey of 20,000 Lutherans, Baptists and Catholics found church youth have a deep longing to belong. Only one out of five youth in church have positive self-esteem. The need for a group of friends and a place to belong ranks high among young people seeking a positive self-image. Some of the priorities of youth in the church are relationships with others (78 percent), to find meaning and purpose in life (78 percent), a closer relationship with God (61 percent), and help in understanding one's self in problems (72 percent). All these needs can be met by a small group of Christian young people and concerned adult counselors. Small group experiences, activities, and trips provided by youth ministry in a local church can mean the difference between reaching a young person for Jesus Christ and that person being lost during the adolescent years.[1]

The minister also can talk about the importance of youth ministry for evangelism and outreach. One of the primary concerns of those who don't attend church is the church's programs for children and youth in their families.

The future of the church will rise or fall on its success with young people, and a continuing flow of information tells us that the following characteristics are prominent among American youth:

● A strong desire to live a good life and an awareness of the need to grow spiritually.

● Sensitivity to injustice and concern over trends toward immorality in society.

● Eagerness for change and innovation—true characteristics of youth.

● Interest in a life of service.

● Influence of religious faith in terms of providing guidance, comfort, and inspiration as well as providing restraint and self-control in personal conduct.[2]

Other information the minister might find helpful to explain the importance of youth ministry comes from USA Today:

"There's a deep hunger among young people for spirituality as evidenced that in (the last year), 64 percent went to church or religious services regularly as compared to only 29 percent in 1974. And the deepest

[1]Merton P. Strommen, **Five Cries of Youth** (San Francisco, Calif.: Harper and Row, 1979), pp. 26-29.

[2]George Gallup, Jr. and David Polling, **The Search for America's Faith** (Nashville, Tenn.: Abingdon, 1980), pp. 114-115.

problems and fears that youth have center on relating with their parents and the nuclear holocaust. Youth ministry can address all these concerns in deeply profound ways, and it is critical for the church to provide ministry and a context for deeper spirituality for youth in the adolescent years."[3]

Financial overview. Next on the formation meeting agenda, schedule another church leader to present a brief (two minutes) financial overview related to the program. During the financial presentation at the parents meeting the church leader can tell about the people who have given money to youth ministry: "We have 10 families in the church that are willing to increase their giving specifically for youth ministry in the amount of $_____. They are making this financial commitment because they believe it is so important."

This kind of commitment will be an encouragement and source of inspiration for the church governing body and at the same time set a good example for the congregation.

Adult youth worker presentation. At the conclusion of the financial presentation, you or an adult volunteer can make a presentation on the purpose of youth ministry in your church. At this time, several themes should be addressed:

● Young people need Jesus Christ for a purpose and meaning in their lives.
● The church is the best place to grow in Christ and to form positive relationships with other young people.
● Teenagers have deep needs for belonging, serving humanity and Christian fellowship that can be met by this congregation.
● The purpose of youth ministry will be to focus on putting Jesus Christ in the center of all that is done and also to provide a place, group and setting within the church for teenagers to meet their deepest needs.

Youth group member presentation. You can give a great deal of credibility to your meeting by having one

---

[3]John Sherlock and Dale Glasgow, "The Mood of American Youth," USA Today (March 28, 1984):1-2a, 4d.

or two teenagers address the parents. The teenagers can talk about what they would like to have happen and what they see happening in the youth ministry. The teenagers can extrapolate on needs and desires for a youth group in your church.

Discussion and forms. After the teenagers conclude their talk, allow about five to 10 minutes for discussion. Then, appeal to the parents to fill out the Parent Volunteer Form to identify what they can do for the youth ministry. This form can be designed in many formats, but be certain that you keep it simple and clear. The more complicated the form, the more difficult it will be for you to use in the future and for the parents to understand. In an initial format, list the kinds of tasks parents could volunteer to do. Here is a sample form:

Parent Volunteer Form

Instructions: Put a check by each item you are willing to do.

_____*Refreshments*
I would be willing to prepare snackfood during the month of _____.

_____*Transportation*
I am willing to help drive on a trip or retreat.

_____*Hosting*
I am willing to host a youth meeting in my home.

_____*Youth work*
I am willing to serve or work on an adult team of youth group sponsors.

_____*Special talents*
I have special crafts or skills I would be willing to share with the youth group such as photography, ceramics, cosmetics, dance, drama or music.

_____*Teaching*
I would be willing to work on a teaching team in our Sunday school.

_____*Vocation*
I would be willing to share with the youth the kind of vocation I'm involved in and explain necessary job preparation.

_____*Other*
I am willing to become involved in youth ministry in the church in these ways: _____

Go over the form with the parents; explain your understanding of each category. Share with the parents some of your kickoff plans and ideas for the future. If you have initial events planned or activities scheduled, relate that to the parents. Also, as further events are planned, continue to keep the parents informed. Especially remember to keep the parents informed of upcoming events in which the parents might want to volunteer or participate (see Chapter 7).

It is important to stress that to be successful, youth ministry must include the parents' sharing of time, talents and resources. Without the parents' participation, they will lose touch with the program and goals. Youth ministry should not become a barrier between parents and their children; it should enhance positive relationships within the family. This can be accomplished through a team approach in which everyone works together.

Closing. Close this meeting by having the participants form a circle and hold hands or put their arms around each other. Conclude with scriptures, songs or prayers that cement the presence of Christ as part of the parents group. Be certain to thank the parents for attending and assure them that you will be getting in touch with them soon to discuss the areas in which they are willing to serve.

ADULT YOUTH WORKERS

In developing a support team, you will need to begin with one or two adults to help you organize tasks and work with you as you initiate youth ministry plans in your congregation. Too large a group of adult volunteers at first tends to be confusing and difficult to coordinate and manage. One or two other adults are essential, however, because you never want to go it alone in youth ministry.

Your formation meeting with the parents probably gave you a good idea of which parents will help you. Also, check with your pastor or other congregational leaders to find if they are willing to assist you in this initial organization. Participation from the church staff will continue to strengthen the youth ministry and also help keep the church informed.

It is helpful for the youth workers to gather and to get to know one another before planning specific activities with the youth. This gathering or meeting of youth workers should be an ongoing experience in which relationships can be deepened. Adult youth workers find it worthwhile to meet once a month and talk about specific responsibilities for upcoming events. You can have different adults responsible for various areas of the youth meeting—such as singing, programming, closing or upcoming events. The adult youth workers then cooperate with the young people assigned to the specific tasks and enable them to follow through on their plans. In working together, these adults develop a close relationship with one another and keep lines of communication open.

When youth workers understand themselves and can communicate clearly time demands and commitments, they work together much more effectively. They will take on assignments and specific responsibilities in youth ministry that best suit them and will be willing to allow other youth workers to fulfill responsibilities without unnecessary guilt or jealousy.

I was involved in one youth ministry effort in which five of the adult workers were so busy with their own schedules that they were too busy to meet with one another. As a result, events and activities were planned without other workers being informed. Conflicts arose, the telephone rang incessantly and feelings were hurt. This happened because the adult youth workers did not meet regularly and talk to resolve priorities and conflicts.

Another consideration is an understanding of the personality type of each youth worker and his or her time demands. One adult youth worker may enjoy and have a lot of time to spend visiting the youth and forming one-to-one relationships. Another adult worker may have such great family or job demands that he or she can volunteer specific times, but is to involved during the week with both family and career to do extra things beyond the evening youth fellowship. As a result, the youth workers need to be aware of the time commitments of other adults.

Young People

In the initial phases of organization, identify three or four teenagers who are interested in having youth ministry in your congregation. Involve these young people on the support team to plan future activities after the parents meeting. Have these teenagers help you build contact lists and make plans for your initial youth events.

Include on the youth support team any adults you have recruited to work with you. The support team of young people and adult youth workers can be expanded into a more formal youth ministry council when your youth ministry is established and has been functioning well for a few months. The youth ministry council then becomes the core of planning and implementation of youth ministry in your church.

It's difficult to establish a recruiting program of adult workers and teenagers when you are trying to start a youth group. Thus, it has to be a part of what happens after the youth group gets going. Once the initial support team members are recruited and working smoothly, take a long look at recruiting future sponsors. This is discussed in detail in the final chapter of this book.

A Starting Time

The support team helps you identify when you want to kick off the youth ministry in your congregation. There are two times of the year that seem to be optimum. The first is with the beginning of the school year in September. The second time is in January, with the start of the second semester. Some churches try to start youth ministry in the summer months. Summer is a good season for youth in terms of free time, but with family vacations and other commitments, it is difficult to organize adequate youth support for activities as well as garner adult participation. I would encourage you to focus either on September or January as a starting time.

Whichever starting date you choose, give yourself a six-month's preparation period. For example, if you are aiming for a beginning date of September:

- In February and March begin to build support with the pastor and congregational leadership, ascertain financial possibilities and develop your purpose.
- Conduct a parents meeting in late spring and work with your youth workers and key teenagers through the summer to build a support team and discuss general plans for the fall.
- In August intensify publicity promoting the youth events for the coming fall. By autumn, everyone should be eagerly anticipating the kickoff.

Be certain that you give yourself enough time to build adequate support and publicize youth ministry. Youth ministry is not like a firecracker—it is much more like a big, thick candle. A firecracker makes a great, loud, wonderful explosion, but then nothing is left. Many youth ministries start with an explosion. Once all the initial energy is expended in the planning and starting stages, there is nothing left to sustain it.

A youth ministry can be compared to the wax in the large candle that will continue to sustain the flame for a long time. With adequate support, youth ministry will take off and glow brightly. Without taking these support steps and giving enough lead time to build a basis, you may quickly extinguish all the energy and not have anything left for the long term. Take the long look. Build a foundation and, on that, your future plans and your organization will succeed.

CHAPTER FOUR
Establish Positive Relationships

Relationships are curious ventures. Unlike a predictable investment such as a passbook savings account, relationships often are unpredictable. Sometimes the energy and emotions invested in relationships simply do not reap what might have been expected. But at other times, relationships reap incredible results.

In youth ministry, relationships with young people are usually the most powerful channels of God's work. Christ becomes alive and real as we see him in others and as they see him in us. Starting a youth ministry requires the adults to start building relationships with the youth.

The initial "push" for building relationships rests with you. This reality struck me a few years ago as my support team was starting a youth group in Lubbock, Texas. We thought the best way to get acquainted with the 150 or so youth in the church was to invite them to a "get-to-know-the-youth-minister" party at church. We sent out 150 post cards inviting them to the party. We got the refreshments ready, decorated the room and waited for all these kids to drop in to meet me.

Only 10 kids came to the party.

I learned the hard way that a post card does not start a relationship. *I* had to meet the young people in their homes, Sunday school, worship and after school. I did not force my friendship on anyone; I catalyzed opportunities for relationships. Before positive relationships can be established, you must first identify the young people who might show some interest in your ministry.

IDENTIFY THE YOUTH

If your church has lacked an identifiable youth ministry program for a long period of time, it may be difficult to determine potential membership within the congregation. To ascertain possible participants, turn to your church office. The minister and church secretary are invaluable contacts in identifying both young people from families who are already in the congregation and any teenagers who sporadically attend church. Find out as much information as you can including the young person's full name, address, telephone number, age, grade in school, and date of baptism or confirmation.

The next source of information is the Sunday school. Ask the class teachers for names and information of potential youth group members. The Sunday school superintendent also might have useful information. If your congregation has a youth choir or music program, talk with the choir director for additional names. Issue a churchwide appeal during Sunday morning services. Include printed forms in the bulletin to be filled out for potential members. The forms should include spaces for name, age, birthdate, grade in school and any other vital information that would be helpful. You also can encourage people to list the names and telephone numbers of other teenagers in the neighborhood who might be interested in participating in a youth group.

The potential youth group members in your congregation can be as young as sixth or seventh grade and as old as twelfth grade. When starting, it is possible to have a wide age range from middle or junior high through high school. But if the group grows to 15 to 20 members, it is important to divide into two youth groups—one for middle school and junior high ages and another for high schoolers.

I served a small county-seat church where our total youth program never grew beyond 10 youth after two years. Size was not important. We had a deep sense of Christian community. Small church youth groups can be

41

very successful with five to six participating youth.

After you have made a list of the pertinent information about every young person associated with your congregation, start contacting the young people. Your strategy should be to contact the most active youth at first, then work down the list to the most inactive.

Make your initial target group to contact the freshmen or sophomores or those in middle school or junior high school, depending on the concentration of young people in your congregation. Older teenagers can be helpful in organizing the program, but generally juniors and seniors in high school are difficult to motivate, especially if they have not been active in a youth program before.

After the youth program has been established and the interested, enthusiastic teenagers have been involved, utilize their help in attracting the inactive young people to the youth ministry. One way to do this is to sponsor a "kidnapping."

Contact the parents of the inactive young people and explain that you and a few of the young people from the group will be arriving to "kidnap" their sons or daughters at an appointed time and that you then will be taking them to a surprise youth gathering. The surprise gathering could be a barbecue, pizza party, swim party, bowling or miniature golf.

Assign one active member to each inactive member. The active members' jobs are to be helpful and friendly to the inactive members and make sure they feel welcome throughout the activity.

Then, all active youth members meet at the church parking lot at a prearranged time and proceed to the "victims' " homes. The victims are surprised and most go willingly to the activity.

If you have a large, inactive group and are unable to kidnap them all at once, plan several other kidnappings in upcoming months.

An added element of surprise to this activity is to have one of the active youth ministry participants dress in costume such as Tarzan or a gorilla. The young person in costume does the actual kidnapping—bodily picking up each victim and carrying him or her to the awaiting car. Outfits can be rented at most costume shops. Check your telephone directory for shops that are close to you.

VISITS

The primary purpose of visits is to establish a positive relationship and to get to know the teenagers. Any other information you might share with them about what will be happening in youth ministry at the church will help establish a good relationship.

Before you begin visitations, make telephone calls and set up appointments with each young person. Ideal times to call on youth include:

● Right after school in the afternoon.

● Immediately after dinner in the evening.

● On Sunday afternoons and evenings, particularly when there are no other youth activities going on in the congregation. This would give you insight into what teenagers are doing on Sunday afternoons and evenings when they are not participating in the youth program.

When you meet with the teenagers, you can either go to a fast-food restaurant and have a soft drink or else visit them in their homes. However, if you go to their houses, be certain to visit with them and not their parents or other family members. If other people in the family get involved in the conversation, after a few minutes graciously explain that you are there to visit the teenager and really want to spend time with that individual. Following are a few suggested areas to talk about to get to know the young people:

● Their school classes and extracurricular activities.

● Special hobbies or sports in which they are involved.

● Their friends and social activities.

● Their room and any kinds of special things that they have such as stereos, computers, video games, photographs, scrapbooks or trophies.

● What they would like to see happen in the youth program.

• Ideas you have for gatherings, events, trips and programs. This will stimulate feedback and give you valuable information.

You also might ask each young person for a school photograph or snapshot, explaining that you are collecting pictures for a church youth ministry card file. Write the teenager's name on the photo to help you better remember the youth. If the teenagers do not have photos to give you, bring your own camera and take the photos of them yourself.

Immediately after each visit, fill out a visitation card with this basic information:

Visitation Card

Name:
Age:
Birthdate:
School: photo
Grade:
School subjects:
Interests and hobbies:
Other family members' names and ages:
Youth group interests and ideas:
Special skills and talents:

I remember a larger church at which I worked; I was charged with the responsibility of trying to involve more than a hundred youngsters in starting a youth program. We had some exciting activities that initially attracted a number of the youth who just wanted to see what was happening. As I began to meet these teenagers, I tried to reinforce the relationships with visits to their homes. I made two or three calls a week and can recall vividly one girl who attended worship services faithfully every Sunday morning but would not come to any other youth activities such as trips, retreats or Sunday school.

My first visit with her gave me a clue as to her problem. She did not want to show me her room, neither did she want to talk about any hobbies or career plans. She was somewhat overweight and badly in need of braces for her teeth. She indicated how self-conscious she felt and how the other teenagers made fun of her and teased her because of her weight and crooked teeth. She was a kind, gentle, sensitive and very shy girl in middle school. I realized that until she built some self-esteem and self-confidence that she never would come to youth meetings.

After my visit with her, I called a number of other young parents in the church and asked them to employ this girl as a baby sitter. I also asked her to baby-sit for my children. In visiting with the other adults, I encouraged them to talk positively to her and to encourage her in attending and participating in church youth events. It was of benefit that one of the other young couples she started baby-sitting for also was working with the youth in our church. By visiting with this girl, forming a relationship with her, encouraging her to do something she could do well, and keeping in constant contact with her, we were able to touch her. She visited a youth event and started attending Sunday school. I encouraged her in a subsequent contact to start in a weight reduction program, which she did using the money she made baby-sitting. As a result, her self-confidence rose and within a year she was in the youth group.

You don't have to make visits by yourself; encourage others to help you. An adult volunteer, youth minister, associate minister, youth ministry adult leader or one of the youth leaders can help you coordinate visits.

Such help with visitation coordination can be meaningful in establishing positive relationships among the adult volunteers and the young people in the congregation. Try to enlist another person to accompany you on visitations as often as possible because this shares the responsibility and also helps keep you motivated.

As an alternative or as a supplement to the visitations, plan a "Blitz Evening." Set aside an evening or two usually just before the youth ministry gets under way and assign adult and teenage volunteers to visit the homes of each young person identified as a potential participant. This should not be an insurmountable task given to a few volunteers. If you have identified 20 or 30 young people that you hope to involve in youth ministry, then each volunteer might be able to visit three or four teenagers each evening and in so doing, all the young people will have contact with an adult leader. The blitz can motivate teenagers to attend an initial organizing event for the autumn or opening session and also give you additional information about the needs and concerns of the young people.

If you're in a smaller setting and only you or one or two others are involved in visitations, consider scheduling a period of intense visits such as in August, early September, January or February. Avoid Christmas, Easter and graduation times.

Whether or not the teenagers you visit come to a youth meeting, the contacts and relationships established can be important in the future. There may come a time when a problem or crisis arises or when an interest develops for youth ministry in these young persons' lives and they will seek you out because this contact allowed them to get to know you. Also maintain at least telephone contact with these non-participating teenagers and seek them out on Sunday mornings so they will know of your continued interest in them. Show this Christian attention even if they fail to show any interest in attending youth activities. This keeps the door open and helps them feel more comfortable should they decide to participate in future youth programs.

After the youth group has met for a couple of months and a pattern of meetings and attendance has been established, it will be easier for you to identify uninterested young people in the congregation who are not yet attending the group. To interest these teenagers, plan another visitation program and utilize the support of the other adult volunteers.

CHAPTER FIVE
Plan a Big Event

After you have made contact with all the young people through visitations, you can formulate ideas for one large initial gathering of all the teenagers—the big event. This big event is to allow time for the young people to meet one another and share the dreams and excitement over beginning a youth ministry. Gather the members of the support team to share the information from the visitation cards. Ascertain the kinds of interests indicated by the teenagers. Note the things the young people have indicated they would like to do, places they want to go and areas they are interested in studying in youth ministry. Also identify those young people most interested in participating in some form of youth group activity.

After the support people have shared, make concrete plans for the big event so that you will spark the interest of the teenagers you met during visitations.

Some ideas for the big event are:

- An overnight retreat at a nearby church camp.
- An evening barbecue at an adult sponsor's home.
- A theme party based on an upcoming holiday or religious event.
- A lock-in. This is a simple, low-cost event that takes place either at a church, gymnasium or home. The youth spend an entire 12 to 18 hours together, non-stop.

Whatever type of big event you plan, be sure to include songs, games, get-acquainted activities, discussion, plans, dreams, worship and devotionals, and a closing time. Allow time for the young people to address the concerns mentioned on the visitation cards. The big event is an opportunity for group members to be together and build enthusiasm as a community.

SPIRITUALITY

In preparing for the initial youth ministry kickoff, it is important that you have your own devotional and prayer time with God. Pray for each young person who has been visited, for your support people and for youth ministry in your congregation. Also, form a prayer chain. Ask your support people and others in the church who aren't directly involved in youth ministry to pray for this event and the young people planning to attend. Develop a strong prayer support for your ministry.

The big kickoff event should provide ample opportunities for sharing, praying and reading scriptures. The first event also should establish a precedent, and if the spirituality of the group is to have a good, solid beginning, it is important that prayer and scripture be utilized in the group from the outset. That doesn't mean the worship has to be heavy and overwhelming. Scripture can be conveyed through pantomiming, creating stories and acting out biblical material. Other creative ways to incorporate scripture include borrowing a video camera and recorder to tape different scenes from scriptures as the youth pantomime or act them out at the start of the big event. Use the video for the worship at the conclusion of the gathering.

GROUP BUILDING

The initial kickoff or big event also should include group-building activities. Group building is simply a process by which people get to know each other, generally through discussions about backgrounds, family members, interests, hobbies, likes and dislikes. Group building can only begin with the one-to-one relationship. A person can't get to know an entire group at once, so start with group building one-to-one, then go to foursomes and then, perhaps, eight in a group, to finally the entire group. Over a period of time, the individuals in the group get to know each other by participating in fun games and get-acquainted activities.

Group building should be a major part of the initial big event as well as in the first few months of youth group meetings. It is important to include at least five to 10 minutes in each of your meetings in group-building and get-acquainted exercises to build positive relationships among the youth. Remember to include group members in all that you do. Any kind of meeting with the youth that only involves one or two people talking at them ultimately will be discouraging. From the outset, the young people need to be involved in the process of learning about one another and building positive relationships with the other adults and teenagers. Getting the young people involved allows the emergence of youth leadership.

PUBLICITY

Publicity is important to ensure that the big event is a success. Every telephone call, poster and post card needs to be done in the best possible manner. Use graphics, catchy themes and other creative devices to saturate the young people with attractive pre-event information. Encouraging the youth to come to the initial event may take numerous personal contacts either at church or through visitations. Begin the publicity at least three weeks to a month beforehand and promote the event extensively so that everyone in the congregation knows a big event for youth is arranged. To accomplish this, be certain that your event publicity includes the following:

1. Make a telephone call to everyone you have visited, explaining the upcoming activity and extending a special invitation.

2. Send a post card to every possibly interested person giving all the details about the event so that both that person and his or her family will know exactly what is to be involved. Generally the church office is willing to send out post cards if you provide the list and assistance in preparing the cards.

3. Create opportunities for the teenagers to register, sign up or express an interest in going to the big event.

4. Make a follow-up call to those who expressed an interest but were not sure if they could attend.

5. Put up posters about the church and publicize the event in the church newsletter and worship bulletin.

If anyone needs a ride to the big event, make certain that he or she has one. Don't let cost become a barrier. If you must charge for the event, keep it to a minimal sum, and if the young person cannot afford to go, the church should try to support the cost.

Following is a checklist for the planning and preparation of the initial big event. Checklists are valuable because they keep you on target and can be used as a reference the next time you plan a similar event.

Checklist for Getting Started

_____Create a master list of potential youth group members. Schedule a time to talk with each person either through a "blitz" or consistent weekly visitations.

_____Visit all the young people on the master list.

_____Enlist support people to plan and pray for the event.

_____Set a date and plan what will happen at the big event.

_____Publicize the big event. Include articles in the church newsletter, announcements in the bulletin, posters about the church, telephone calls, post cards and an opportunity for all to register.

_____If necessary, provide transportation for the youth.

_____Conduct the big event. Include sharing, games and recreation, Christian input and inspiration, worship and prayer. Ascertain current needs and interests by involving participants in general plans for future events and programs.

_____Organize the thoughts and future program ideas spurred in the discussion time.

_____Join with others to pray for a successful youth ministry.

I cannot overstress the importance of keeping checklists when planning an event or an activity.

One summer I was working with four youth ministry interns in a large congregation. These interns were undergraduate or seminary students. The five of us were planning a retreat by a lake, and each intern had an assigned responsibility.

In the planning stages I had emphasized: "Now, make a checklist of all the things that you need to do and all the materials you need to have. Be sure to include people who you want to contact about various responsibilities and have a time block so that each day as you approach the event, you know exactly what you want to do next."

Three of the interns took to heart my suggestion. They made a detailed checklist and as they accomplished each task, made each telephone call, and gathered each resource, they checked it off. The fourth intern was responsible for the food. She went shopping, saying that she could remember everything she needed. She soon returned and sure enough, everything was there which to her seemed to be proof that a checklist wasn't needed. We gathered the food, loaded it into the van and went to the lake. As we were unpacking and setting up for the first evening meal, the intern ran to me and said: "We've got a real problem. I forgot the meat."

All the hamburgers and hotdogs had been left in the kitchen. She hadn't needed a checklist at the grocery store where everything was on the shelves, but as we loaded the van, it would have been helpful to make certain all food items were included. It was an interesting meal that evening—hotdog and hamburger buns, baked beans, salad and dessert—but no meat.

Suggested Big Event Schedule:
A Lock-In

FRIDAY

9:00 p.m.   Gather at a gymnasium, home or church
for group-building exercises and games.
"How Are You?" is a fun get-to-know-you

activity.[1] Station two of your leaders at the door as your group arrives for the big event. The first leader asks each young person, "Hi, how are you?" The second leader writes the response on a 3 × 5 card and tapes it to the member's back.

When everyone has arrived, split the group according to answers. All those with cards reading "okay" form one group. Those with cards reading "fine" will make another group and so on.

Next, each group is assigned to create a skit on the meaning of, "Hello, how are you?" Present the skits and discuss how sincere people are when they greet each other. Conclude this game with each young person going to others and meaningfully giving a verbal or non-verbal, "Hello."

10:00 p.m. Brainstorm for future youth group activities. This is an optimum time because the participants now have known each other a little while and are willing to indicate some of their interests and needs. Go over ideas of possible activities that were mentioned when the youth filled out their visitation cards before the big event.

If this is a new youth ministry, gather suggestions for meeting times. The ideal schedule is to meet weekly to build continuity. However, semimonthly meetings also give members a steady type of contact and basis for growth.

At the end of this chapter is a list of program themes, recreational ideas and possible service projects for the big event. From this list, the young people can select ideas, issues, program topics and events that seem interesting. As suggestions are

---

[1]Thom Schultz, ed., **More . . . Try This One** (Loveland, Colo.: Group Books, 1980), p. 66.

made, write them on a blackboard or newsprint. After the big event, this modified list of activities can be used to develop a detailed schedule for youth group meetings.

11:00 p.m.   Break for refreshments. Prepare a pizza, make ice cream sundaes, play a new game or relax together.

11:30 p.m.   Show a Christian film or video. (Check with your denominational office for church libraries or catalogs that carry names of Christian films and information to order the film.) Or use this time for a videotape of an outstanding movie that can be discussed before going into more games.

SATURDAY

12:30 a.m.   Keep up the enthusiasm by initiating fun and games. This is the time, if you're in a gymnasium, to play a lot of different games such as volleyball or basketball. If you're in a church, use a fellowship hall for active tag games or relay races.

Generally, lock-in participants stay in the same building for the full 12 to 18 hours. Going to another site can break the closeness that has been established. If your group decides not to actually "lock themselves in" to one room for the full length of the big event, you may want to go midnight bowling or roller skating.

Whichever you decide to do, this time should be an activity or fun period—nothing requiring serious thinking or concentration.

3:00 a.m.   Spend a peaceful time together for worship or sharing. You also can show other videos or play more games, have food or snacks, and allow those who want to sleep to do so.

6:00 a.m.   Get everyone up to help prepare breakfast. Afterward, go on a sunrise walk.

8:00 a.m.   Conclude the lock-in by conducting a worship and songs. The participants then can go home and sleep.

Note: Lock-ins are best conducted on a Friday evening rather than a Saturday night that might leave the participants too tired to attend the Sunday morning worship service.

PROGRAM THEMES

Bible study: miracles of Jesus; meaning of the cross; death and resurrection of Jesus; disciples; early church; Palestine in Jesus' day; world of the early Christians; parables of Jesus; lives of Old Testament people (David, Job, Joseph, Moses, Joshua, Noah, Jonah, Esther, Ruth, Solomon); life of Paul; women of the Bible; prophets and prophecy; history of the Israelites; Beatitudes; Bible themes (salvation, faith, hope, joy, love, spirituality); life after death; end of time; the patriarchs (Abraham, Isaac, Jacob); and study of a book of the Bible.

Relationships and values: building a Christian group; self-identity; dealing with emotions (anger, jealousy, anxiety, frustrations, joy, fear); building relationships and friends; dealing with parents, teachers and other adults; accepting and understanding oneself; making decisions and handling conflict; coping within the family; meaning of the church; making personal decisions and morality; Christian sexuality (love, sex and dating); forgiveness; becoming Christian leaders in the church; learning the workings of the church; psychology and the Christian; peer counseling; and building affirmation.

Express faith through art: dramas and plays; music (starting a singing group or producing a musical); dance; art (trips to museums or creative art projects such as banners); puppetry; and clowning.

Spiritual growth and disciplines: meaning of Christianity; Christian freedom; witnessing and sharing of faith; studying God; praying; meditating and devotionals; gifts of the Spirit; fruit of the Spirit; opportunities of stewardship; fasting; methods of Bible study; meaning and purpose of worship; developing personal faith; and growing in Christian love.

History: history and beliefs of the Christian church; beliefs and histories of other denominations; history of other faiths (Hinduism, Islamism, Buddhism, Confucianism, Judaism); religious sects and what our faith can say to them (Church of Jesus Christ of Latter-day Saints, Christian Science, and the occult); historical periods of religion (Early Reformation and Holy Wars); prominent figures in religion (Martin Luther and John Wesley); missionary work; seasons (Lent, Advent and Pentecost); and the future of the church.

Issues: science and Christian faith; environmental concerns; war and peace; government and how it affects us; welfare programs; international affairs (hunger, Third World, racism and bigotry, nuclear arms control); problems of runaways; alcoholism; substance abuse; pornography; careers and vocations; death and euthanasia; capital punishment and criminal justice; and technology.

Fun activities: swim party; trip to a park or amusement center; roller skating, bowling or pizza party; lock-in; sports event such as softball, volleyball or basketball games (either to attend or in competition with another church or within the church).

Service projects: visit shut-ins in their homes; visit the elderly at a nursing home; go to a children's or orphan center; develop a clown ministry for evangelism or visitation; visit the pediatrics ward in a hospital; do a work project at the church; plan a work project or summer workcamp trip; participate in a food drive for world hunger; and collect canned goods for a food bank or any particular needy project that your congregation supports.

CHAPTER SIX
Organize Your Youth Ministry

Now that the big event has been conducted and the young people have been excited and enthusiastic about the possibilities of what's going to happen, it is important to take the proper organizing and planning steps for youth ministry. It is tragic when enthusiasm and hopes build at the initial event, but afterward nothing happens.

MAINTAIN MOMENTUM

The people who planned the big event and others on the youth ministry support team need to determine details of youth activities. As we mentioned earlier, the youth ministry support team consists of adults working with the young people, interested young people, Sunday school teachers, music leaders and church staff related to youth ministry. Be sure to include the whole team in determining a schedule.

The young people at the big event gathered general ideas for social events, study topics and outings. For the next three months it is the job of the youth ministry support team to plan and schedule ways to meet these expressed interests. For example, if the young people are interested in building positive relationships with one another, the support team could plan the following for the first month:

First meeting: Show a film on dating relationships.

Second meeting: Do a group activity based on starting and ending relationships.

Third meeting:	Plan a recreational outing such as a pizza party, roller skating outing or pool party.
Fourth meeting:	Form a panel to discuss "How to have a Christian date and pick a Christian partner" or "The do's and don'ts of dating."

If the young people expressed interest in the history of your church or other churches in your community, the support team could plan the following for the second month's activities:

First meeting:	Collect your church's scrapbooks and old photographs. Create a time chart of your church's history.
Second meeting:	Invite a pastor and long-time member to share their experiences and beliefs.
Third meeting:	Invite the pastor or youth leader from another church in town to share its history.
Fourth meeting:	Visit the other church.

Perhaps the young people expressed a desire to learn more about Jesus and his disciples—how they reached out to others in their ministry. The third month could include the following:

First meeting:	Do a Bible search of the Book of Mark to find all names and titles of Jesus. Use Bible reference books to look up the meanings. Make banners or posters highlighting your favorite name of Jesus.
Second meeting:	View a film or video on the life of Jesus. (See your denominational or Christian film catalog.)
Third meeting:	Invite a mature Christian from your congregation to share his or her faith in Christ.
Fourth meeting:	Play Picture Charades with stories and parables of Jesus' life. The youth group splits into small groups

of three or four with one leader
each. The youth leader calls aside
the small group leaders and tells
them a parable. The leaders return
to their groups and draw a clue to
the parable. No talking is allowed.

When youth ministry first is started, it is best to plan
ahead and to have the youth ministry support team
meet at least once or twice a month to plan, evaluate
and organize the specifics of the upcoming meetings.
Burnout tends to afflict those who "wing" meetings by
planning in one short hour before the meeting.

The support team also should plan so that each
meeting includes:

● Songs and games.
● Sharing and other group-building activities.
● Heart of the program such as Bible study or discus-
sion on that week's theme.
● Closing time for either worship or devotion.

Specific schedules enable the people who are going to
be responsible for each meeting to know exactly what's
going to be done or needs to be done.

It is important that the youth ministry team appoint
one person to prepare or secure resources for upcoming
programs and schedules. This "resource" person gath-
ers information for each week's topic using books, liter-
ature, music, film catalogs and any other available
data. The resource person then reports the ideas to the
youth ministry support team and works with them to
prepare programs. The resource person can obtain catalog addresses from Christian bookstores or denominational publishing houses.

In these first few months, it tends to work out that
the adults on the support team do most of the planning
for the youth group meetings with a few young people
assisting them. As time goes on, however, more of that
planning responsibility gradually should be transferred
to the young people until they prepare most of the youth
group programs.

Establish a Youth Ministry Council

It now is time to move into the vital step of making the youth ministry an ongoing entity. The support team should be instituted officially in the church so that congregation members recognize the team's contribution to the total life of the church. The support team has an ongoing responsibility to maintain the youth ministry in the church and to be answerable to the entire congregation. You may want to change the name from youth ministry support team to youth ministry council as official recognition of its being established in the church. As the youth ministry council is recognized, it is a good transition time to involve others to work on the council and thank those who are no longer able to continue serving.

The Planning Event

Once the support team has guided the group for a few months and the youth ministry is established, it is time to initiate another large group activity—the planning event. In most churches with ongoing youth groups, the most effective planning strategies use these units:

Time Blocks
January to May
June to August
September to December

A planning event should be scheduled one month before each time block.

The youth ministry council organizes the planning event in which all the youth have the opportunity to select programming ideas. The youth also should have an opportunity to serve on task forces to implement programs, events, trips or lock-ins.

Following is a checklist of necessary steps for the youth ministry council to take for a planning event involving the youth group:

Planning Event Checklist
1. The youth are given an opportunity to list ideas and interests for activities at the big event.
2. The youth ministry council meets to redefine and condense the list.

3. The council then writes a calendar which notes preplanned dates such as seasonal and traditional church events.
4. The youth ministry council brainstorms three or four program ideas for each possible topic including Sunday evening programs, recreational events, retreats, lock-ins, trips and service projects. Utilizing the basic list of program themes at the end of Chapter 5, the youth ministry council can come up with a number of ideas that specifically fit the needs of the young people. The purpose of program themes is to get you started—not to set limits on possibilities for youth ministry.
5. The resource person takes ideas to the council for inclusion in programming options.
6. Program ideas, recreational possibilities, trips, retreats, special events and happenings are typed for presentation at the general planning event.
7. The youth planning event is scheduled and organized so that everyone knows when it will be, how much it will cost, how long it will be and the overall agenda.
8. The meeting is publicized so that the maximum number of young people will attend.
9. The registration and final preparations are made for the event.

DURING THE EVENT

The council presents the different ideas and the participants vote or select the most popular ideas.

Young people are asked to volunteer to work on either the task force responsible for presenting specific program topics, in planning events or service outreach.

It is important that an adult be part of each task force as this helps ensure that the work will be done, that the effort will be made with consistency and that the congregation remains informed of the project.

It now can be seen why one person cannot do all programming and planning. As previously emphasized, the leader needs everyone's help to support youth ministry in the church. In a small group, two or three adult sponsors may be adequate, but if a youth group grows beyond 20 to 25, it is important to have four or five adults support and sustain the program. A reasonable rule is to have at least one adult for every six or seven young people in the group; this sustains the necessary relationships and the essential program support for ongoing youth ministry.

I still recall images from my first planning event which was attended by about 30 junior high youth. The meeting seemed like mass chaos as we tried to accomplish all my plans. Junior high youth were running everywhere. I had forgotten that anything left unlocked in the church will be explored by a young teenager. I finally rounded up the teenagers and started the meeting. The planning time to choose ideas and concepts for future study was reduced to absolute confusion. We had divided everyone into groups of three or four putting either a youth leader or an adult in each small group for an evening of brainstorming ideas. An entire blackboard was filled with suggestions—one of which was a trip to Disney World in Florida. I was in a state of shock. I simply was trying to plan youth meetings for the fall, not organize a trip from Texas to Florida. Yet, this was high priority for them, and I could see that they really wanted to go. So, we planned to take a trip a year later, giving us enough time to raise money for travel and other expenses.

I was excited by their plans, but overwhelmed by their dreams. Nonetheless, we went to the parents meeting with the plans to go to Disney World, and the parents were so enthusiastic that they decided to help raise the funds for a chartered bus which they thought would be safer than church vans or rented vehicles.

It was a great, exciting time for the young people because they were going to do something big that they had never done before.

In the course of trip from Texas to Disney World in Florida and home again, we played games, activities and learning exercises. We also spent two days on the beach in a spiritual discipline retreat that enabled the youth to develop a closer relationship with Jesus Christ. Of the eight days of travel, the teenagers spent only a day and a half at Disney World. However, I cannot begin to measure the amount of positive relationships and spiritual growth that happened on that retreat. Two young people who had never attended anything at the church before were led to Jesus Christ. Others who were only marginally interested in the youth group became solid members and participants. All this came from an idea at 10 o'clock on a Friday night in a chaotic junior high planning meeting. That idea spiritually changed 30 young people and brought them into a deeper relationship with Jesus Christ.

In the same way, as the youth ministry council initiates a planning meeting with the youth group, some program ideas will be met with great success and some activities will be met with failure. But that's part of youth ministry.

Using the information gathered from the planning event, a calendar then is completed with the youth activities listed in detail including the dates for each program and the volunteers for each task force. The calendar should include other relevant dates such as: school events, athletic meets, choir rehearsals, church ceremonies and special denominational conferences.

Youth Ministry Calendar

February 5

6:00 p.m.	Snack supper. Parent volunteers: Mr. and Mrs. Brown
6:30 p.m.	Songs, announcements, group building. Leader task force: John, Bill, Jean
7:00 p.m.	Film on dating.
7:30 p.m.	Discussion of film. Dating task force: Jay, Joan, Barbara
7:50 p.m.	Closing worship and circle. Leader task force: John, Bill, Jean

February 12

6:00 p.m.	Snack supper. Parent volunteers: Mr. and Mrs. Hanson
6:30 p.m.	Songs, announcements, group building. Leader task force: John, Bill, Jean

7:00 p.m.   Program, "Making or Breaking Up." Dating
            task force: Jay, Joan, Barbara
7:50 p.m.   Closing worship and circle. Leader task
            force: John, Bill, Jean

February 19

3:00 p.m.   Swim at indoor pool. Recreation task force:
            Jill, Carol
6:00 p.m.   Pizza party.

February 26

6:00 p.m.   Snacks. Parent volunteers: Mr. and Mrs.
            Williams
6:30 p.m.   Songs, announcements, group building.
            Leader task force: John, Bill, Jean
7:00 p.m.   Program, "College Panel on Dating." Dating
            task force: Jay, Joan, Barbara
7:50 p.m.   Closing worship circle. Leader task force:
            Joan, Bill, Jean

All task forces include the young people and adults who have volunteered earlier during the planning event to study, plan and present the program.

PUBLICIZE THE CALENDAR

After the youth calendar has been planned, it needs to be checked and approved with the appropriate staff and church leaders. When plans are made months in advance, it is necessary to communicate and compare with the church calendar and other church group activities to avoid conflicting schedules. It then is important to publicize events on the youth calendar through the following means:

● A weekly post card to all the young people and adults involved.

● A weekly or monthly newsletter.

● Announcements in the church worship bulletin.

● Articles and announcements in the church newsletter.

● Telephone calls to different young people and adults before the events.

INFORMATIVE PARENTS MEETING

The parents should be kept informed and involved as much as possible after the planning event. This is best accomplished through another meeting with the parents.

To get the parents to attend this meeting, send written invitations with a letter describing the group's plans and needs. Use a letter similar to the one described in Chapter 3. Send these a few weeks before the meeting. Follow up with telephone calls to confirm their intentions to attend. If the parents are unwilling to attend, adults involved in youth ministry can try to schedule a time to visit those parents and communicate the need for their support. Most parents will want to attend the meeting and the few who don't may be impressed that someone is concerned enough for them and their teenagers to visit and share all the plans.

Also, extend an invitation to the parents of young people who are not members of the church, but who regularly attend the youth group. This can become an exciting outreach and evangelism possibility for the church.

The parents meeting can begin with a potluck for both parents and young people, after which the young people can go to a youth group meeting and the parents can meet with the adult leaders. Give the parents the youth group calendar of activities that evolved from the planning event. The parents can volunteer for such tasks as preparing snack suppers, chaperoning at events or providing transportation as indicated on the calendar. Adapt the volunteer forms described in Chapter 3.

The parents meetings are special times in which parents communicate to the youth leaders their concerns or criticisms of the youth program. These can be dealt with honestly and constructively, and conflict can be resolved before it undermines the work of youth ministry programs.

In all the years I have had the parents meetings, I never have had an event canceled because of lack of parental support. However, should you not receive enough adult volunteers, some events will have to be canceled.

IMPLEMENTATION

After the parents are aware of the upcoming activities and have volunteered, the resource person needs to help the task forces review the calendar and plan detailed programs for each study topic.

Although the task forces can generate much of their own planning for special events, retreats, lock-ins, recreational activities and other happenings, someone has to be knowledgeable of the available resources and data. Again, that individual is the resource person, who should prepare a packet for each meeting and list all the ideas and books in which the information was found. Thus, as the task forces begin to plan the program, the resources are readily available.

The task force must schedule a time to meet to go over the program, review suggested resources and assign responsibilities. (See the end of this chapter for program suggestions the task force might want the resource person to research.) When you schedule that meeting depends on your group.

You might find with your young people that you need to meet at least a week before the program to review the resource person's ideas and map out the meeting. However, it often is difficult for many young people to work another youth meeting into their busy schedules. Because of this, one of the best times to work with the task forces on the evening program is the afternoon beforehand. If the youth program is on Sunday evening, then gather before the snack supper to go over the basic ideas. (A snack supper is a light and inexpensive meal. Parents and other adult volunteers plan each menu and its preparation. A snack supper is an added fellowship time to the upcoming program for the evening.)

If the group meets on a weeknight, consider meeting with the task force for an early dinner and afterward work on the program presentation. By meeting in the afternoon on the day of the program, the youth can be more motivated to get program details accomplished because of the time pressure involved. Another reason to schedule the task force preparation for the program a few hours before the meeting is so that the meeting will be fresh in the task force members' minds.

The youth ministry council should regularly evaluate all plans and potential problems. Any change in schedule, fund-raising projects or conflicts should be discussed by the youth ministry council. The council also should review revisions in the way the fellowship is taking place. This means that before any problem gets out of control, the youth ministry council will meet and deal with it directly. This monthly meeting also provides time for prayer, sharing, growing and any ongoing training that may be needed. It is important to continually coordinate the work of the youth group through the youth ministry council.

Communication

Maintain regular contact with the teenagers, not just those doing the program and the task force planning special events, but also with all youth participants. Weekly post cards, newsletters and telephone calls need to be done. The key people to do this are those on the youth ministry council. To help keep everyone informed, assign each member of the council the responsibility of contacting certain youth group members. This can be done on a regular basis through telephone calls. Such a system establishes a way to let members know that they are important to the group, they're missed if they can't attend, the group cares if they are sick, and someone is there to pray and care for them.

Remember, it takes time to organize and plan for a long-term youth ministry. It can take two to three years to get all the factors in place. Give the group time to increase in size, and as it grows, to build a foundation, get organized, and find and meet the needs of the young people in the congregation. Take a long-term approach to youth ministry to ensure the support and planning necessary so that the youth ministry in your congregation not only will thrive but also be a commitment to the future young people of your church.

PROGRAM SUGGESTIONS
FOR A TASK FORCE TO DEVELOP

Program #1: Making and Breaking Up

1. Tape large newsprint on a wall, label one section "Men" and the other "Women." Divide into small groups of three to four men or three to four women.

2. The small groups discuss—
    Men—Great lines we use to impress women
    Women—Great lines we use to impress men

3. Write the answers on the newsprint. As an entire group, discuss which lines work and why. Which lines build the self-esteem of the other person and which are pure con? What lines would the men add that girls have used on them? Which lines would the women add that guys have used?

4. Re-form small groups and discuss—
    What lines do guys use to break up after going steadily with a girl? What lines do girls use to break up? Discuss the responses and write them on the newsprint. Put a plus sign by those that are positive and which would allow the girls and guys to remain friends. Place a minus sign by the destructive remarks.

5. Each group next discusses the good reasons for breaking up and writes these on the newsprint.

6. Now discuss in small groups—
    What qualities do you seek in a date?

7. As a total group compare the answers and then work through the items discussing if the group members agree or disagree.

8. List on newsprint the following ways couples might break up and decide the most Christian and loving way:
    ● Write a letter
    ● Make a telephone call
    ● Ask a friend to tell your date that "it's over" and give back the ring

• Stage a fight and then use the fight as an excuse to break up

• Ask someone else on a date, making sure your old date finds out about it and then will feel compelled to break up with you, saving you the dirty work.

• Meet face-to-face and talk it out leaving as friends

9. If time permits, have the group role play the preceding approaches.

Program #2: For Whom Would You Die?

1. Put a check next to the person for whom you would give your life. (Prepare handouts or write on a blackboard.)

_____Best friend

_____Family member

_____Another Christian

_____An enemy

_____An important or famous person (president, governor, movie star)

_____An important belief or ideal (freedom, the nation)

_____A needy stranger

_____A casual acquaintance

_____A person in distress

_____Other (explain) _____

2. Rank the items on this list from 1 to 10, with 1 the person you most willingly would die for, 10 the person you least willingly would die for. (Review the manner in which the young people answered these.)

3. Read Romans 5:6-10 to the group. As a group, discuss which people in the preceding list Christ would die for. Discuss in small groups the difference between the way the young people marked the list and the manner in which Christ might have answered. Did Jesus have any assurance or guarantee that if he died on the cross that anyone would believe in him as Lord or Savior? If you died for someone, would it make any difference in his or her life? What guarantee would you want?

4. In a closing worship, distribute miniature silver pocket crosses to each person in the circle. (Check with a nearby Christian bookstore or your denominational catalog to order these crosses.) Sing a song such as "Were You There?" Ask each person to look at the cross and complete as a closing thought: "Jesus died for me because" . . .

CHAPTER SEVEN
Take the Long Look

A recurring theme in this book has been the need for support in youth ministry. In starting a group, it is necessary to earn support from the pastor, several youth, the congregation and adult volunteers. After the initial adult volunteers are recruited and the youth ministry is running smoothly, you will need to establish a program for developing adult workers. Recruitment and development of adults and support people should remain a significant objective and long-term commitment. Many youth workers serve only 18 months. The need for developing new adults is fairly obvious.

RECRUITING ADULT YOUTH WORKERS

Utilizing other adults to work with you in the youth ministry is known as the *Team* Approach. The qualities to look for in adult volunteers for your team remain fairly consistent from congregation to congregation. Here are some checkpoints to consider when recruiting:

- Strong faith in Jesus Christ
- Positive self-image
- Well-liked and accepted by both young people and other adults
- Realistic views about young people and youth ministry
- Follows through on commitments
- Has the time to build positive relationships with the young people

A few comments can be made about these qualities. A person cannot give what he or she does not have. If the adult is to be a role model of the Christian lifestyle, then that person needs a strong, personal relationship with Jesus Christ. It also is important for a person to have a good, strong self-image. Often it seems that adults become involved in youth work for ulterior motives. The adult may have strong emotional needs. As a result, that adult will use the youth to meet his or her needs for love and affection. Or the adult may believe that the young people need to be "straightened out" or "brought into line." The volunteer may have certain negative myths about teenagers and be seeking to work with the youth group solely to correct the supposed problems. Such motivations and unfounded misconceptions can be destructive to relationships with youth.

Adults also need to have a demonstrated record of working well with other adults. Because youth ministry requires not only working with teenagers but also having the youth ministry function as a part of the total church ministry, it can require negotiation and compromise on the part of youth workers so that the program calendar and budget fit into the total program of the church.

Self-identity also is important for the volunteer. The person working with teenagers who feels good about himself or herself tends to build healthier relationships with group members.

It's difficult to evaluate self-image without doing some introspection. An adult wanting to volunteer can fill out the following characteristics list to see if he or she needs an improved self-image.

Self-Image

Underline any words that apply to you:

- A nobody, life is empty, a somebody, life is fun
- Stupid, bright, incompetent, competent, naive, sophisticated
- Guilt, at peace with self, horrible thoughts, pleasant thoughts, hostile, kind, full of hate, full of love
- Anxious, panicky, relaxed, cowardly, confident,

unassertive, assertive, aggressive, friendly
- Ugly, beautiful, deformed, shapely, attractive, unattractive, pleasant, repulsive
- Depressed, happy, lonely, wanted, needed, unloved, loved, misunderstood, bored, active, restless
- Confused, full of pleasant thoughts about past events
- Worthwhile, sympathetic, intelligent, considerate

Go over the list and put a plus mark by those underlined words that are positive and a minus sign by those words that are negative. Review the list to see if there is a tendency toward positive or negative traits and if there is a good or bad self-concept.

If the adult volunteer made an overwhelming negative response, view this as an opportunity to work with that adult in a counseling, pastoral, loving way to help him or her see the strengths instead of focusing on the weaknesses. The self-image problem needs to be improved before the adult is encouraged to work with the youth group.

AGE

Before recommending an adult work with the youth group, also consider his or her age because each age group offers certain strengths and benefits.

Young single adults (18 to mid 20s): highly energetic, close enough in age to young people to understand many of the pressing problems, enthusiastic, often have the time to be deeply involved in youth activities, positive role models for the next stages of development for the youth.

Young marrieds (18 to early 30s): Positive role models for Christian relationships with youth, more time and energy necessary to relate to young people and their activities, enthusiastic and energetic for youth activities.

Mid-life couples (late 30s to late 40s): Possible surrogate parental relationships with youth, understand adolescent problems from the perspective of being parents, viable interest in youth ministry because it affects their own children.

Mid-life single adults: Likely surrogate parents because don't have their own immediate family, more free time in personal life.

Single-again adults: Relate positively to young people who may come from homes with parental turmoil or breakup, can relate to the specific concerns of youth facing this type of crisis, may be seeking to develop an extended family and nurturing group that would involve them in positive relationships with other youth.

Empty-nest adults (40s to retirement): Desirous of building new relationships and keeping in touch with young people, based on positive experience in raising adolescents and understanding the need for adults to relate in affirming ways to adolescents, increased time in personal life that can be used with young people.

Retired adults (late 50s and older): Ability to be more tolerant and patient with young people, capacity to be surrogate grandparents, greater time with less job or career demands.

When recruiting volunteers, it is important to find adults of varied ages and lifestyles so that the youth can benefit from your team. Qualities are more a determining factor than age. Commitment and willingness to learn and work with youth are obviously important overriding factors.

PERSONALITY

Every personality is important in working in youth ministry. That is why a team approach is so essential—it allows more people than just yourself to be involved, and the more personalities, the broader the appeal. The purpose of team ministry is not just to support you or broaden the base of people who can take on tasks and responsibilities—it also is to give the teenagers other personalities they can relate to or view as role models. Everyone relates to certain kinds of personalities. Considering the number of youth you will meet with, not all are going to relate to your kind of personality. Even though you are well-liked, not all the young people will see you as a person with whom they can share their deepest concerns.

I once participated in a youth ministry team that consisted of three couples. The wife in one couple was dynamic, outgoing, friendly, fun and well-organized. She was at ease in front of a group as well as behind the scenes, making plans for everything that happened. She was dependable and enthusiastic. Her husband, however, seemed to be just the opposite. He was quiet and reserved with a good, dry wit. He enjoyed one-on-one encounters. He certainly would not get in front of the group or plan and organize a retreat. He liked things on the spur of the moment. I best remember his choice in clothing, for he only wore two kinds of clothes—dress jeans and boots or work jeans and boots. In west Texas (where we were), he was comfortable with those church members who saw themselves as cowboys. In a few words, he was easygoing, spontaneous and relaxed.

All the teenagers who were well-organized, excited about what we were doing and right in the thick of things related to his wife, but the youth who were not quite into the organized youth ministry and who didn't see themselves planning programs, leading the group, or setting up service projects, related to the husband. The husband would sit in a corner with five or six of the guys in the group who also were cowboys and they would make jokes and enjoy the event in their own way.

The important aspect of this was the husband's work with the teenagers. He was building relationships with those youth. From time to time, in the middle of cracking a joke or talking with the guys in the corner, he would look up and say: "Did you hear that?," or "I wonder what that means," or "Golly, I didn't know that." And the guys who were just goofing off would look up and say: "What happened? What was he talking about?" What this adult youth worker was doing was calling attention to things that were important, and because he was building a relationship, the guys around him started listening because he was and started asking questions because he did. As freshmen, those guys had started off in the corner making jokes and having a good time, but by the time they were seniors, they were leaders, officers and organizers both on the local and district level in youth ministry. He had related to them

74

and their needs. Everyone is needed and can contribute
in youth ministry.

TIME

Another word of advice regarding recruitment of
adult volunteers—set a specific term of service so that
the adults won't get burned out. Congregations have
found it helpful to encourage adults to be involved in
youth ministry at least two years but no more than
three years. If the adults serve at least two years, they
will be able to build good relationships with the other
adult volunteers and also with the young people. This
also gives the adults adequate time to build knowledge
and experience.

Another purpose is served in the two- or three-year
arrangement. For the first year the adults are in an ap-
prentice or intern stage, learning from the other adult
volunteers. This first year also is the time to build relationships. The youth workers then use the second and
third years to impart this knowledge and experience, to
take leadership and to train the new volunteers. After
the third year, time and energy demands usually neces-
sitate the adult volunteers quit youth work—even if just
for an interim. Structure the adult volunteer program so
that the adults can quit easily and gracefully without
feeling guilty or remorseful and also feel free to return
to youth work at another time.

APPROACHES FOR RECRUITMENT

There are several approaches to recruiting adult
volunteers. One is the Council Approach. The youth
ministry council seeks people who best fit the needs of
the youth ministry and who have the qualities necessary
to work with youth. Based on the initial screening and
discussion, the qualities are prioritized and a list is
written. Drawing from this list, the council gets names
of potential volunteers to be visited by members of the
youth ministry council.

A letter describing what is going to be discussed at
the visit and a profile of what the youth worker is ex-

pected to do is sent prior to the visit. It is important to write a profile of the volunteer and his or her duties. In this way the person understands the time commitments and can make a decision based on what is actually expected instead of on hearsay or past experience.

The letter to the volunteer is followed with a telephone call arranging a visit from the representatives of the youth ministry task force. One or more representatives of the council then go to the potential volunteer and spend an evening talking with him or her about youth ministry in the congregation.

This face-to-face visitation is an opportunity to answer questions and describe the youth ministry philosophy. Encourage the person being recruited to pray and seriously consider the opportunity. Do not force the adult into volunteering. To avoid the need to pressure volunteers, recruit early. If you need a volunteer for the fall, talk to potential sponsors in the late winter or spring.

Another approach to recruiting adult volunteers is the *Group Approach* in which all youth ministry council participants, young people and adults in the church are invited to an orientation session to define all that is expected in youth work and learn details of the youth ministry—its purpose, goals and specific objectives. These people then are given the opportunity to ask questions before volunteering.

Encouraging potential volunteers to ask questions in the group setting often allows people to feel more comfortable and open and can cover concerns that some have but are hesitant to ask. As you close this meeting, ask all attending to pray about commitment. Contact each person within a few days to find if he or she is ready to make the commitment to the youth program.

I have successfully used both Council and Group approaches in my congregational youth ministry and have been especially excited about the Group Approach. One spring I asked more than 40 people to attend an orientation meeting for youth ministry. Most of those who attended had never been involved in youth work. The congregation had built an image of recruiting one or two people to work with each group and then leaving them with the responsibility until they were totally worn out. Adults became unwilling to volunteer because of the feeling that they would have to sacrifice too much time and energy. Youth ministry had not built a good reputation because it was leaving a trail of burned-out adults.

As we invited adults to attend this orientation meeting for youth ministry, we assured them that no strings were attached and no commitments would be asked. We presented youth ministry in a positive manner. Young people expressed their needs and desires for youth ministry after which adults shared their own positive experiences, frustrations and personal reservations about youth ministry.

After this candid presentation, adults were able to ask questions. The meeting opened youth ministry in a realistic way to them. Following this meeting we asked the adults to pray and consider the possibility of serving for the next two years in youth ministry. When we later contacted these adults, more than 20 agreed to be on the youth ministry team. This was an exciting time in the life of the congregation as youth ministry moved from being a one- or two-person martyrdom to a team ministry that met the needs of both the young people and the adults.

Master Volunteer Checklist
For Starting a Youth Ministry

Let's take a moment to explore the specific steps for starting or reviving a youth ministry.

_____I understand my decision and calling to do youth ministry.

_____My motives are positive and centered on Christ and others.

_____I know what I do best with youth.

_____The purpose of youth ministry in our church is clearly understood; I've worked the purpose through with the
    _____Pastor   _____Youth leaders
    _____Church leaders   _____Parents
    _____Other adults working with youth

_____I have a support group of young people and adults assisting me with the tasks of youth ministry.

Name   **Type of support**

_____   _____

_____   _____

_____   _____

_____   _____

_____   _____

The amount of money the church has budgeted for this is $_____.

_____I have met with the parents and recruited volunteers to help.

Parent(s) name   **Support task**

_____   _____

_____   _____

_____   _____

_____   _____

_____The list of potential youth is compiled.

_____The big event (initial youth gathering) is:

      _____Planned

      _____Adult and youth supported

      _____Publicized (letters, telephone calls, announcements)

      _____Follow-up scheduled

_____Upcoming month(s) schedule is:

      _____Meeting needs of youth

      _____Supported by resources, money and volunteers

      _____Coordinated and cleared with church calendar

      _____Okayed by church leadership and pastor

_____Monthly youth council meetings are scheduled and conducted

_____Planning events are scheduled for the year

_____Parents are informed of future activities

_____I have a plan for building a youth ministry resource library.

_____I am maintaining positive and growing relationships with others in my spiritual walk with God.

_____My family is informed and consulted of my schedule and remains high in my priorities of time commitment.

_____My prayer partners with whom I can share are:

_____

_____

_____

IS YOUTH MINISTRY WORTH THE EFFORT?

We have been exploring the specific tasks involved in starting or reviving, planning and organizing youth ministry in a congregation. Is it worth it? Perhaps in telling a story, I can emphasize the importance of youth ministry.

A teenage girl in one church I served rarely came to youth group meetings, yet mysteriously appeared at every trip or retreat. She had many problems with morality and drugs. As a result, her attendance at trips and retreats often would jeopardize the program we were trying to do and positive ideas we were trying to communicate. Her influence was negative on the group and many discipline and relational problems were caused by her attendance. Parents were concerned that her presence was detrimental to the entire group and often hesitated to allow their children to attend events at which the young lady might attend.

The first major retreat of the year was particularly important for the ongoing life of our group and much rode on its success. This teenage girl decided to attend, and I was deeply worried about her negative influence. My anxieties were borne out. She caused many problems within the group, yet she seemed attentive at each session and appeared to want to participate, though her behavior remained destructive. I had numerous confrontations with this young person throughout the retreat and was beginning to wonder at the end of the weekend if all the work, planning and turmoil in youth ministry was worth the effort.

In the lodge in which we were staying we had hung a "warm fuzzy" clothesline. On it were clothespins for each attendant. During the course of the retreat, people would write "warm fuzzy" notes of affirmation, caring and love. During the retreat everyone received lots of notes attached with their clothespins, and at the end of the retreat everyone retrieved the notes to take them home. As I took the line down, my clothespin held a solitary note. Not paying much attention, I put the note in my pocket, packed up the clothesline and headed toward the church van. Immediately before I left I read the note, which said, "I accepted Christ this weekend."

That cryptic note was signed by the troubled girl that had been such a problem. Quite frankly, I didn't believe it. Thinking it was another one of her cons, I dismissed the thought until the end of the following week. I learned through a conversation with other youth in the group that the girl, the following Monday morning, had gone to her school counselor's office and stated: "I need help. I really want help. Can you help me?" She voluntarily went to a Christian halfway house for drug rehabilitation and over the next six months got off drugs and began a life alive and vibrant for Jesus Christ.

This teenager's life, its dramatic change, and all the struggle that went with it confirmed for me then, and continues to remind and affirm for me now, the great value of youth ministry. You may never know how significant your touch, empowered by Jesus Christ, will be in the lives of the youth with whom you work. It may take years before the young people ever realize how important you were in their lives. But Jesus Christ needs you. He needs you as his voice, as his touch, as his presence with youth.

Philippians 4:13 says:

"I can do all things in him who strengthens me."

Proceed in youth ministry with the knowledge that Christ is with you and strengthens you every step of the way. With that assurance and tremendous power, you can start or revive a youth group.